From the Hood To the Church

Inspired by True Events

DeMarcus Brewster

DEDICATION

First and Foremost I must give thanks to Jesus Christ who is my Lord and Saviour. Without having Jesus in my life, I wouldn't have the courage to tell my story to the world. I would like to thank my Proverbs 31 wife Alicia Brewster and my children whom have shown strong support for me throughout my entire life-changing journey. I would like to thank my church family at Twins Rivers Church in Saint Louis, Mo. for their support. Finally, to all my family and friends who is supporting me by reading and sharing my story, thank you. I truly appreciate you all from the bottom of my heart.

To everyone in all walks of life, no matter what life throws at you keep God first.

CONTENTS

CHAPTER 1

FOSTER CARE

I remember running home from school excited to tell my great great auntie that I aced my test. I made it in the house, and told her the good news! She was excited and very happy for me. I remember her giving me so many hugs and kisses. She just kept on reinforcing that I was smart and that I can do anything I put mind to. By this time, she was getting up to start cooking dinner. She said she was gone make me something extra special for doing so good in school. Now I'm so excited, happy, and feeling so confident in myself.

As I'm about to wash up for dinner I heard a loud knock at the door. That knock was louder and eerier than I ever heard before. So I instantly ran to see who it was. I saw this tall white man in a brown uniform and a white lady dressed up like she was about to go to church. I soon realized it was a police and a caseworker. Then I heard the caseworker say I had to go with them. They were there to take me away. It felt like a ton of bricks hit me in my chest. I couldn't breath. My head started hurting and I felt so confused and sick.

My great great auntie refused to let me go and demanded to know why. By this time the police intervened. He stated it was an anonymous phone call and I must take him away. I didn't understand why this was happening to me because my great great auntie made sure I was taken care of. She made sure I ate three meals a day and most days she walked me to school. I was good where I was at! I didn't have a lot of materialistic things but I was overflowed with love. I didn't want to go so I started trying to get away, I ran as fast as I could but they caught me. No matter how hard I tried to fight to get free, I just wasn't strong enough. " I mean what do you expect from a eight year old child." I just remember sitting in the back seat of the police car crying so bad and feeling the worst pain I ever felt. I loved my great great auntie!

After I was put in foster care my auntie became maniacally depressed. She withdrew from the world and subsequently died from a broken heart. It still haunts me to this day not knowing who called the authorities and turned my life upside down. This was the beginning of my nightmare and rebellion.

So how did I get here? Sadly, I was in foster care all of my childhood. My birthmother had eight children. She couldn't take care of us because her life was consumed with drugs and alcohol. She gave birth to me and didn't want me so she left me in the hospital. My great great auntie came to the hospital and picked me up. I lived with her and my other two brothers until that dreadful day. Three of my siblings went to live with a foster family in Cahokia, IL. One of my sisters lived with different family members throughout her life and my last sister remained in my birthmother's home.

I had become a child in the system. My foster mother quickly adopted me and my two younger brothers. We were now Brewsters. After a "checkup" visit to the white lady in the church clothes, I became very angry. I didn't want to see her ever again and wanted to do something that would hurt her. After the meeting, I left with my foster mom and stole my caseworkers pager. I was mad and all I wanted to do was go back to my auntie! I went with my new foster mom and I remember optimistically thinking, "Yes, I know things are going to be good." We loaded up in her van and I felt somewhat happy and excited at the thought of being treated good. My caseworkers pager beeping over and over as we pulled up to her house abruptly interrupted my thoughts. I stole the pager and when asked about it, I lied. I snapped back to reality and didn't care about anyone but my auntie.

I remember my foster mom was stealing money from me as I walked in on her after school. Even though she was stealing from me I was the one that got beat for the whole ordeal. The money that the state was giving her for me was not being used for me; it was getting used for drugs, alcohol, or anything else that didn't concern me. I had to turn to the streets to get money, love, and guidance.

I started selling drugs at a young age just

to buy myself clothes, shoes, hygiene stuff, and even food. I thought I was going to a happy healthy environment but everything that glitters ain't gold. This home was no better than where I was before. In fact, it was worse. How can an eight year old be depressed? This feeling lingered well into my early adulthood. I didn't understand that word at the time but I knew I wasn't happy. I would often see other people in a happy family free of abuse and neglect and get envious. I wanted that life and often questioned God why I couldn't I live that way. I just thought about the way my life was going and I felt like I had no future. They should've just left me where I was at.

I was on the road to self-destruction. I was being exposed to drugs, women, alcohol, guns, and fast money. I hung with the wrong crowd and everywhere I went it seemed like trouble followed me. I started coming in the house all hours of the night, usually after smoking weed and drinking with my friends from the projects. I hated coming to this house because there was so much chaos and drug abuse it felt like a crack house.

I was ashamed of my life and I hated it. I was so sad and depressed I tried to take my life. One evening I took a wire hanger, unraveled it, placed it around my neck and began to try to squeeze the life out of me. My next attempt at taking my life was throwing myself down a flight of stairs in an attempt to break my neck and back. I felt no one would miss me. Needless to say my attempts didn't work. Thank God He interceded and I'm alive and well! What I didn't know then is that I've got a purpose for my life. Once I realized I couldn't change my situation I started to make the best out of it, until it was time for me to remove myself out of the situation.

Even though I was going to church under her roof I never had a real relationship with Jesus. I'm happy that he always had me under his wings because things would definitely got way worse before they got better. What really took me to the lowest point in my life is in foster care was when another man molested me and sent my mind and body in a world of confusion.

CHAPTER 2

MOLESTED LEADS TO A DOUBLE LIFE

Foster care was really hard for me at times. It opened a door for me to be molested by another man who I trusted and considered a friend.

It happened when I was a teenager and at a time when I was most vulnerable. I went to his house as a safe haven and to get away from home. The first time it happened, I remember suddenly waking up out of my sleep with this mans hand down my pants. I jumped up and was shocked and confused at what was going on. He was remorseless. He stood right over me and laughed as if it was a joke and okay. He told me not to say anything. He promised me clothes, shoes, money, and even a car if I didnt.

I didn't like what happened to me and would not have told anyone even if he didn't tell me not to say anything. I was too ashamed and I feared being judged or called a faggot. In my adolescent mind, I felt like getting these materialistic things were an adequate tradeoff especially since I didn't have it.

Things got out of control. I was actually taken advantage at his house multiples times. Not just by him but also by other men he knew. A man was fondling me while I was sleep. I woke up angry and punched him in the face. I thought to myself, what did I do for this to continue to happen. This man I trusted let other men try and have their way with me. The shoes and the clothes were not worth it anymore.

The trauma of being molested by another man shifted my mindset. It had me thinking that messing around with men was the thing to do to get things I wanted.

Living a double life started when I was twenty years old and homeless in the streets of Saint Louis, Missouri. I had a job at a local bar that wasn't paying enough to makes ends meet or even pay rent. I couldn't survive and it caused me to sleep on the streets. Often times I would find myself sleeping on benches and even cold concrete steps of a church right in Saint Louis. I would lay my head down and try to figure out how I was going to get through the next day.

The money I earned from my job was only enough to cover my habits. I needed more money, so I found myself dealing with men to get the things I needed. The bar I worked at had a lot of homosexual men that came in there all the time which made it easy to open that door.

One night after I got off work, a guy who was a regular in the bar approached me and asked what I was about to do. I told him nothing and I was about to go "home" and get some rest. I got in his car and instead of going "home"; we ended up in a dark alley where things that happened seemed all too familiar. This was the onset to a two-year span of my sexuality confusion that led to a double-life.

After work, I would stay in abandoned buildings but it got so cold some nights in the fall an winter that I would use men for a safe place to lay my head.

When I was living this double life I never did anything for free. It was basically just a means to an end. Even though I was engaging in homosexuality I was still engaging with women. In the beginning of my relationships with women I was honest with them that I was living a double life. They accepted me and didn't judge me, or so I thought. Many of the women I was dealing with were bisexual themselves. We would often talk about threesomes but never engaged in it. I was getting deeper and deeper into lust because I wanted to do it. It was going to happen if I continued down this path.

After a while, these same women eventually would start to judge me. They were engaging in same sex activities just as I was, but I was different in their eyes. I didn't care about how they felt about me and continued to live my life the way I knew how. For a while I was back and forth between men and women trying to fill a void. As I continued to deal with men, my life was starting to spiral more and more out of control. I felt like I was losing my mind! I had to watch my back all the time. All I knew was that I wanted to find me. During this time, I lost myself and contact with reality.

I remember sitting on the porch with a few men then all of sudden bullets started flying past my head! Two people that were sitting on the side of me got shot! I was shot at for hanging with the wrong crowd! Fortunately God put his shield of protection up and I was not harmed. I can now tell my story and let people know that if you want deliverance from living a double life there is a way out.

Being exposed to homosexuality at such a young age, I didn't really understand that it is an abomination to God! After getting to know God, I knew that He was the only way I could be healed! You have a choice, which God calls free will. I'm free from all desires of being with a man for over twelve years and counting. God did it for me!

CHAPTER 3

DRUGS, ALCOHOL, AND SEXUAL ABUSE

At a young age I was exposed to the street life, drugs, and alcohol. I tried hard to stay away from it and go to school. I was being pushed to stay in school. I just kept seeing the street life and how you can make money in it. I was poor growing up, so I became fascinated with seeing so much money. Eventually I started to skip school and hang out in the streets.

Getting in that street life, I was introduced to different types of drugs. First drug I was introduced to was marijuana. The crowd I use to skip school with and hang out in the projects with smoked marijuana, so it was easy for me to be exposed to it. I went from just smoking with them and eventually I started buying it on my own. I was fifteen when I started smoking marijuana, so everybody wouldn't sell it to me. One thing about the streets is you still had those dealers who was all about a dollar and would sell to a kid.

I went from buying ten dollar sacks to ounces just to stay high. Sometimes I would match blunts with my homeboys. I didn't smoke with just anybody so it all depended on who was around. I recall it being five of us and we all had two blunts. We decided to match, and we smoked all ten of them. It got to the point where I wouldn't do anything if I wasn't high. It was almost like I needed it to function.

On the days I attended school I would wake up early in the morning, get dressed and go stand on the corner and get high before I caught the bus to school. During school hours I would leave during gym class just to smoke and sneak back into the building before the next class. Once school was out that's when the fun began for me. I would smoke until it was time for me to go home later that night.

My foster mom was always telling me to stop coming in my house high, but I never listen to her. Before I went to work I would go to the projects to smoke before it was time for me to catch the bus to work. It got so bad that I would steal money from work just to support my marijuana habit. I decided that it was time to give up this habit because it drove me to start stealing money from my job. I gave up marijuana and got introduced to codeine and ecstasy pills by a family member. Being in the streets gave me access to different spots to get codeine and ecstasy pills. These drugs were kind of expensive, so I had to get in a life a crime to support my new habits.

Working a nine to five wasn't enough. The codeine was expensive because you needed things to mix with it to complete it. When I smoked marijuana it was everyday, but doing codeine and ecstasy pills was not an everyday thing. It was more like three times a week. When I did these drugs I was always in the house or with the family member who introduced it to me. I did it three times a week, but I would abuse it to the point where I was like a zombie. I know you probably seen zombie movies on TV and how slow they were going. That's how those drugs had me, so I would always make sure I was in a safe zone.

Most of the time I would abuse it to the point where I would fall asleep and wake up not remembering anything. I remember a point of time while I was doing codeine and ecstasy pills, I started back smoking marijuana. At times I felt like a junky, because of the drugs I was consuming in my body, but I had an "I don't care" type of attitude. I loved the feeling the drugs gave me and if I was facing problems it would all fade away.

These drugs would give me memory loss, so I didn't remember what I was going through at the moment. I was so high that I would wake up the next day feeling the same way. I was under the influence of drugs and alcohol which led to a lot of sexual activity. I had a mindset that I needed drugs and alcohol to perform sexually, so every time it was time for me to commit a sexual act I would call the dealer or stop by the liquor store to get a bottle of alcohol. Being on drugs and alcohol gave me a hypersexual drive and all the time I was trying to fill a void.

In the midst of all these sexual sins I was committing there where ungodly soul ties attached to me. Ungodly soul ties is a dangerous thing and you wonder why are you doing things you never did before. The more I had these sexual encounters with different partners, eventually their problems became my problems.

I had to stop all this! The turning point for me to stop codeine and ecstasy pills was hearing about people I know or hung out with overdose on this stuff. That put fear in my heart and mind thinking I could be the next person to overdose from this junk, so I stopped.

I just thank God for delivering me from drugs, alcohol, and ungodly soul ties. It's been three years and counting since I did any type of drugs and drank any type of alcohol. As far as ungodly soul ties, I don't have to experience that because I'm happily married to a beautiful and amazing woman of God.

CHAPTER 4

MEETING MY WIFE IN THE MIDST OF CHAOS

The first time she called I ignored her! I really didn't feel like being bothered. I was walking to the projects looking for some weed to smoke and had no time for anyone or anything else unless they were supporting my habit. I met up with one of my homeboys to get my mind right, He had exactly what I was looking for. It was just another day for me, getting high and not caring about anything else. I had my fix.

Moments later, I noticed my phone ringing again. This time it wasn't a call I wanted to ignore. It was my "home girl". I went ahead and answered it. She had a job for me to do. Her voice on the other end was refreshing and just what I wanted to hear. The job was to go do a drug run but instead of selling the product, we were going to rob their crew. I knew I was going to make some fast money and I definitely needed some quick cash. I was all in! After a short conversation I told her my location and within minutes she was there to pick me up. She wasn't alone. She had another chick with her and one of the homies or at least I thought he was. My "home girl' filled us in on all the details. All I had to do was hold the gun on the person and they will take care of the rest. The way it sounded seemed like it was going to be easy money. Not realizing that everything comes with a price, I overlooked the possibility of what could go wrong and its consequences.

I hop in the truck with them and I yell to my homeboy that supplied me with my daily dose of weed "I'll be right back, I gotta go handle some business." I said "don't worry, when I get back we'll be straight and drinks will be on me. During the ride we were smoking, popping pills, and talking about the plans for this robbery. It should be simple and sweet.

The person who we were going to rob was going to a party so we had to go to a store and get some clothes. My 'home girl' was a very good booster, so that was the plan before the big event. We were going to go get some fresh clothes, go to the party and at the end of the night rob ole boy and leave. So now we're on our way to the store and the driver and I are passing the gun back and forth checking it out to make sure it was ready for war.

Finally we made it to a clothing store and that's when things took a turn for the worse. We all went into the store to find some clothes to put on except for the other chick that was with us. She was under the influence of drugs and alcohol and while we were "shopping" getting ready for the party, she was in the parking lot doing donuts. Security realized that was the truck we got out of. With her causing all that attention they called the police. After being in the store a while, we had all the items we went in there to get but we started to get a really bad feeling. We then realized we were being watched. We immediately put everything down and hit the door. The police questioned and frisked us. We didn't have anything and they were about to let us go. I began to praise the Lord!

Trying not to panic, I wondered why a cop was running towards us? I figured it out shortly after I heard on the police scanner, "We found a pistol in the truck!!" So the homie I thought was my friend says "Man why didn't you tell me you had a gun in my truck?" I felt like a ton of bricks hit me!! They instantly put us in cuffs and as we walked outside it was like a movie scene with the police lined up like we robbed a bank!. Now my mind is racing a million miles a minute like what am I'm about to do now, am I really about to go to jail? I felt confused and lets be honest somewhat angry. How did this happen? Here I am 18 years old, in the back of the police car on my way to jail with a gun charge! Unfortunately, I never made it back to my homeboy to give him those drinks I promised or to return the phone call to my future wife. That would all have to wait until I served my time.

It was my first offense, which was also a felony. I spent 6 months in St Clair County jail and after my release, I had 1 year of probation. During my time served, I was able to reflect on the decisions I made. I wanted to change my ways. I wanted to stop doing drugs, drinking, and robbing people. My mind was made up. I was going to get out of jail, find a job and live right.

I thought life was hard before, but it was harder now than ever before. Job application after job application came with rejection after rejection. No one wants to hire a felon. No one would give me a chance. All I wanted was to do the right thing. Strapped for cash, I had to turn back to doing what I knew for quick money. I picked my gun back up and started robbing, and hanging with my old "homies" again.

In the mist of my difficulties, I managed to return that ignored phone. Although we had chemistry, life had different plans for both of us. We didn't commit to a relationship and we both went our separate ways. God had a plan and 12 years later I would call her my wife.

CHAPTER 5

JAIL AND REVIVAL

It's been many times that I had a turning point in my life. I remember a time when I was just chilling in the hood on a good summer day and one of the homeboys came and swooped me and some of the homies up. We grabbed some alcohol to drink and some bud to smoke. If I'm not mistaken it was on a Good Friday. We were riding through the city stunting while drinking and smoking. All of a sudden we ended up in some projects chilling with a couple of females we just met. Everything was going good and in the blink of and eye the situation took a turn for the worse.

My homies and I were sitting inside the car on cloud nine. One of the homies had to go to the bathroom so he hopped out and crapped next to the driver's door. We all laughed at this practical joke. All I know is I was under the influence of alcohol and marijuana and I wasn't in my right state of mind. When it was time to go, the driver stepped in it and he went crazy. I remember the driver hit the gas and took off backwards in the car with all of us in it doing a hundred miles per hour. We hit a hill and the car started flipping. I remember telling God with my eyes wide open please don't let me die like this. God spared all of our lives that night. *R.I.P to one of my homeboys who died in a separate situation.

The car was totaled but it was still drivable. We all should have died that night the way that car was looking. We pulled back up in the hood and the homies was like what happen! I told them the story laughing. I made a mockery of the situation. That night I also made an empty promise to God that I was done with the streets and I'm going to church to serve him.

The thing about that is I accepted Christ in my mind, but not in my heart. That turning point didn't last to long. I went to church maybe once or twice and back to the streets I went.

I remember times of being in the hood and a small voice would tell me to leave. Most of the time I would walk off to go home and relax for a while after hearing that faint voice.

One time I abandoned my friends and hours later some of the homies called me and told me how they just got shot at by people they were beefing with. Good thing I wasn't there because I was loyal to my crew. I stayed ready for war with a pistol under my belt. But what if I was there? I would have shot back, potentially killed someone or gotten killed myself. The Lord removed me from that situation so I can observe what could happen to me. He was working on my soul to serve him years later.

Funny thing is, God always kept his hands around me. To this day most of the people I hung around with are dead or in jail. This might sound crazy to whoever is reading this, but being placed in jail from time to time saved my life. Doing time behind bars saved me from the fate of perishing in the streets like a lot of people I knew.

My spirit was dead and was not connected to God. He didn't give up on me and revived me. He gave me another chance in life to find him. Remember in life you have good days and bad days just remember keeping God first through it all is the smartest decision you can ever make. My life took many turning points in which I learned from in the end.

CHAPTER 6

SAVED BY GRACE

My life has been a roller coaster from the very beginning. I spent a lot of time hanging in the streets and that led to a life a crime. A life of crime led to me being in and out of jail from the age of eighteen. I moved to Indianapolis, IN to remove myself from the environment I was in. I wanted to leave the streets alone but I learned hanging around the same people doing the same things will not get you a different result. It'll eventually lead to jail or six feet under. I wanted to start fresh and get away from it all.

I was sharing an apartment with roommates in Indiana and circumstances were finally starting to look up. This was until the moment when Federal Agents showed up at my doorstep. This would be the final time I went to jail. It was for student loan fraud. The gig sounded simple. I would apply for student loans, get the money and have a quick come up. However, I didn't apply for the loan, my friend did and he used my name. I agreed with this once but what I didn't know is that he continued to apply for loans using my name in multiple states. I found out when Federal Agents came and got me from Indianapolis and transported me back to Saint Louis, Missouri. I soon learned that I owed $50,000 worth of student loan money I never saw. I didn't have money for a lawyer and with my record, who would believe it wasn't me? However you look at it, I was guilty! I was sent back to jail.

This time I was incarcerated for 9 months with 3 years probation. During this time, and I built a relationship with the true and living God who resides in heaven. Me and some other inmates started having bible study daily. This didn't come without pressure from other inmates. Often times I would have to avoid fights because I read my bible and wanted to be invisible to those that didn't share the same agenda. I will confess, it was hard not to fight especially with my background. I knew these encounters were nothing but the devil because I was finally getting closer to God.

During bible study each person would take turns opening us up in prayer. We all came from different walks of life, but we all had one thing in common which was building a relationship with God. Most of the times we just talked about the bad things we did in life and if it wasn't for the grace of God we would have not made it. To be honest if it wasn't for God keeping his hands on me and connecting me to the right people I would've been dead.

I didn't really watch TV a lot while I was locked up. Most of the time I was reading my bible, praying, or sleeping. While I was resting, God was giving me visions concerning things about my life, which was scary at first.

Before I was locked up, I had not seen or spoken to my foster mother in years. God showed me in a dream and a vision that I was going to get out and go back there and make things right between us. By the grace of God that vision came to pass. I reached out to one of my brothers and he got in contact with her.

After I was released she let me move with her
but I had to get there. I walked nearly 50 miles
from St Genevieve, MO to Arnold, MO. Once
I finally had the opportunity to use a phone, I
called my brother. He picked me up from
Arnold and dropped me off at my foster
mother's home in Washington Park, IL. I am
thankful we have restored our relationship and
we are best friends today. After all we've been
through she took me back in.

I prayed a lot and asked God for a wife
and to bless me financially. During my release, I
got settled at my foster mothers house. I found
a job, a church to attend, and by the grace of
God he blessed me with a janitorial job. Things
were finally starting to get better for me.

I met a female I thought was the one and
I began to have sexual intercourse with her
before marriage. "Let's have a baby first, then
build a relationship with God," she said to me. I
felt that was a tactic of the enemy (Satan
himself)! This went against everything I was
standing for in Christ. I just wanted to get
closer to God when I was released from jail. I
was a carnal mind Christian that was fed up

with the whole fornicating thing, so I cut the relationship off.

After all that sinning God still had his hands around me. I got back in contact with my homegirl I mentioned in chapter four. We started hanging out and I would always talk to her about the grace of God. We were on the same level and had the same spiritual desires. She was a key part in my life that found its way back to me. She completed me!

A couple weeks later I moved out of my foster mothers house. We moved in together and got married a few weeks later. I know it may seem fast and abrupt, but I knew she was the one. She has unquestionable faith in God and accepted me for who I was.

Years later and counting we are still together and serving God together. It doesn't matter what you're going through in life. If you want to be kept by God he will keep you. After all of the carnal things I did after my release, I was still saved by the grace of God.

My walk with God got even stronger and becoming a pastor is my passion. No matter

what you go through in life you must trust and
keep God first to get the results you want.

CHAPTER 7

TRUSTING GOD-REFLECTION FINAL CHAPTER

Chapter 1 Reflection: When I first was placed in foster care it was so hard for me to understand why I had to experience this. Then I realized this entire ordeal was a Wilderness Experience God took me through to get to the Promise Land that came many years later in my life.

Chapter 1 Reflection Scripture: Philippians 3:13-14(NIV) - Brothers and Sister, I do not consider myself yet to have taken hold of it. But one thing I do: Forgetting what is behind and straining toward what is ahead. I press toward the goal to win the prize for which God has called me heavenward in Christ Jesus.

Chapter 2 Reflection: When I was younger, being molested opened up doors for perverted sexual immorality. I was living such a wicked and immoral life. Deep down inside I knew this perverse way of life was totally wrong. I was wrapped up in sin and complete darkness. I didn't know how to escape. As things started falling apart in my life, I started wondering about a way to escape and that's when Jesus Christ started to reveal himself to me.

Chapter 2 Reflection Scripture: Leviticus 20:13(NLT) - If a man practices homosexuality, having sex with another man as with a woman, both men have committed a detestable act. They must both be put to death, for they are guilty of a capital offense.

Chapter 3 Reflection: Foster Care played a big part in my life getting exposed to drugs, alcohol, and sexual abuse. Facing so many problems in the foster care system I would turn to drugs and alcohol to forget all about the pain I was going through. Most of the time I was under the influence of drugs and alcohol, so it was hard for me to control my hormones. I wanted more and more sex trying to fill a void. Not knowing getting to know my Lord and Saviour Jesus Christ was the only person who could fill that void.

Chapter 3 Reflection Scripture: 1 Corinthians 6:9-10(ESV) - Or do you not know that the unrighteous will not inherit the kingdom of God? Do not be deceived: Neither the Sexual Immoral, Nor Idolaters, Nor Adulterers, Nor men who practices Homosexuality, Nor Thieves, Nor the Greedy, Nor Revilers, Nor Swindlers, will inherit the Kingdom of God.

Chapter 4 Reflection: As a born again believer I had to realize that God created the end of my story first and then he created the beginning last. Not knowing the person I was getting in trouble with God has already ordained to me Mrs. Brewster.

Chapter 4 Reflection Scripture: Proverbs 18:22 (NKJV) - He who finds a wife finds a good thing, and obtains favor from the lord.

Chapter 5 Reflection: Submitting to authority wasn't something I did freely. My disobedience caused me to be placed in jail. Once I got the revelation to submit to authority that was placed over me while in custody, my life took a turning point. I started to hear God's voice more clearly. He would speak to me through words, dreams, and visions. He revived my soul and molded me to His image to help win souls for him.

Chapter 5 Reflection Scripture: Romans 13:1-5 (NLT) - Everyone must submit to governing authorities. For all Authority comes from God, and those in position of authority have been placed there by God.

So anyone who rebels against authority is rebelling against what God has instituted, and they will be punished.

For the authorities do not strike fear in people who are doing right, but those who are doing wrong. Would you like to be without fear of the authorities? Do what is right and they will honor you.

The authorities are God's servants, sent for your good. If you are doing wrong, of course you should be afraid, for they have the power to punish you. They are God's servants sent for their very purpose of punishing those who do what is wrong.

So you must submit to them to, not only to avoid punishment, but also to keep a clear conscience.

Chapter 6 Reflection: God had a big plan for my life that's why he placed me in police custody. He knew I needed to sit still for a while so He could speak to me. He knew that was the only way to get my attention. Once I realized God saved me by His grace my life was turned around.

Chapter 6 Reflection Scripture: Romans 6:14 (NIV) - For sin shall no longer be your master, because you are not under law, but under grace.

Chapter 7 Conclusion: The mistakes I made in my life had me thinking that my future was dark and there was no hope for me. I am still experiencing the affects of some of the decisions I made while in the streets. I became a convicted felon and that made it almost impossible to find a decent job. I've spent most of my adult life on probation. This meant I could not leave the state and had to ask for permission to do so. I couldn't receive a passport, therefore I missed family vacations and forfeited my $145 I used to apply for it. I have $50,000 worth of student loan debt a "friend" caused me.

I remembered what Jeremiah 29:11(NIV) says - For I know the plans I have for you," declares the Lord, "plans to prosper you and not to harm you, plans to give you hope and a future." That's when I came to conclusion that God was really with me.

Most of the things I went through in life and made it through, was God's favor over me. He kept me when I didn't want to be kept. I understood what Romans 8:28 (NLT) meant- And we know that God causes everything to work together for the good of those who love God and are called according to his purpose." I am a living testimony. Everything I went through in life was God's plan for me.

ABOUT THE AUTHOR

DeMarcus Brewster was born in Centreville IL on August 30, 1986 at Centreville Township Hospital which later became Touchette Regional Hospital many years later. He was born to Cora Simms who passed away in 2018. His father was Johnny Morris according to what he was told by my family members. He never met him and his whereabouts are unknown. He spent most of his childhood growing up in Brooklyn, IL and in East St. Louis, IL. The things he did in those streets could have gotten him killed, but God always spared his life. Defying any statistics against black boys in the streets, he graduated form Curtis Miller Alternative High School in Alorton, IL on May 22, 2005 with a 3.6 G.P.A. He was put into foster care at the age of eight and was later adopted by his foster mother. His last name suddenly changed from Simms to Brewster. DeMarcus' trials and tribulations were all part of Gods plan for his life. He is a married man who loves his wife and 5 children (3 girls and 2 boys) and enjoys spending time with them. He rededicated his life back to God three years ago and was baptized on April 28, 2019.

"Becoming a Pastor is my passion. I want to reach the souls that have never heard of Jesus Christ. I am not looking back until that goal is accomplished!"

2 Corinthians 5:7
Live by Faith and not by Sight

Psalm 34:18
The LORD is close to the brokenhearted and
saves those who are crushed in spirit.

Matthew 11:24
Therefore I tell you, whatever you ask for in
prayer, believe that you have received it, and it
will be yours

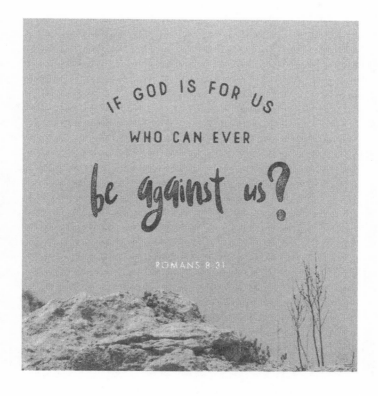

IF GOD IS FOR US
WHO CAN EVER
be against us?
ROMANS 8:31

From the Hood to the Church